THE STORY OF THE MIAMI HEAT

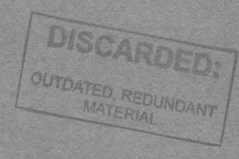

THE NBA: A HISTORY OF HOOPS

THE STORY OF THE MIAMI HEAT

SHANE FREDERICK

CREATIVE
PAPERBACKS

Published by Creative Paperbacks
P.O. Box 227, Mankato, Minnesota 56002
Creative Paperbacks is an imprint of
The Creative Company
www.thecreativecompany.us

Design and production by Blue Design
Art direction by Rita Marshall
Printed in the United States of America

Photographs by Alamy (Peter Phipp/Travelshots.
com), Corbis (DARREN HAUCK/Reuters), Getty Images
(Issac Baldizon/NBAE, Victor Baldizon/NBAE, Andrew
D. Bernstein/NBAE, Nathaniel S. Butler/NBAE, Lou
Capozzola/NBAE, Angelo Cavalli, Jesse D. Garrabrant/
NBAE, Barry Gossage/NBAE, Andy Lyons/Allsport, John
W. McDonough/Sports Illustrated, Fernando Medina/
NBAE, Layne Murdoch/NBAE, Greg Nelson/Sports
Illustrated, Bob Rosato/Sports Illustrated, Jamie Squire),
Newscom (FREDERIC J. BROWN/AFP/Getty Images,
Robert Duyos/MCT), USA Today Sports Images (Mark J.
Rebilas)

Library of Congress Cataloging-in-Publication Data
Frederick, Shane.
The story of the Miami Heat / Shane Frederick.
p. cm. — (The NBA: a history of hoops)
Includes index.
Summary: An informative narration of the Miami Heat
professional basketball team's history from its 1988
founding to today, spotlighting memorable players and
reliving dramatic events.
ISBN 978-1-60818-436-1 (hardcover)
ISBN 978-1-62832-023-7 (pbk)
1. Miami Heat (Basketball team)—History—Juvenile
literature. I. Title.

GV885.52.M53F73 2014
796.323'6409759381—dc23   2013039305

CCSS: RI.5.1, 2, 3, 8; RH.6-8.4, 5, 7

First Edition
9 8 7 6 5 4 3 2 1

Cover: Guard Dwyane Wade
Page 2: Guard Dwyane Wade
Pages 4–5: Guard Jason Williams
Page 6: Guard Mario Chalmers

TABLE OF CONTENTS

WARMING UP 8

A TEAM GROWS UP 16

ONE HOT RIVALRY 22

TROPICAL TITLES 30

INDEX 48

COURTSIDE STORIES

BECOMING THE HEAT 11

THE EXPANSION CHAMPIONS 21

SHORT-HANDED BUT ON TARGET 24

BIG FIGHT, LITTLE COACH 29

PARTY OF THREE 32

NOT JUST FOR SKATERS .44

INTRODUCING...

GLEN RICE 12

RONY SEIKALY 15

PAT RILEY 18

ALONZO MOURNING 27

DWYANE WADE 35

LeBRON JAMES 43

WARMING UP

MIAMI IS SEPARATED FROM THE ATLANTIC OCEAN BY BISCAYNE BAY AND MIAMI BEACH.

The region surrounding the city of Miami, Florida, is known as the Gold Coast. With some of the warmest weather and most beautiful beaches in the United States, it is a popular destination year-round for vacationers from all over the world. A glamorous city famous for its art, music, and fashion scenes, Miami also enjoys its sports.

Up until 1988, however, the city was strictly a football town, dominated by the Miami Dolphins of the National Football League and the University of Miami's college football team, the Hurricanes. But sports fans in southern Florida were eager to root for a team in another sport. In 1988, the National Basketball Association (NBA) gave Miami fans that new professional franchise. Because Miami's tropical temperature plays such a prominent role in the life and identity of the city, the new club was named

9

SOUTHERN FLORIDA HAS A REPUTATION FOR BEING SUNNY AND VACATION-FRIENDLY.

the Miami Heat.

At the time the Heat were born, the NBA was thriving, thanks largely to the appeal of superstars such as Boston Celtics forward Larry Bird, Los Angeles Lakers guard Magic Johnson, and Chicago Bulls guard Michael Jordan. To take advantage of this boom in popularity, the NBA decided to expand from 23 teams to 27. The expansion occurred in two phases: the Charlotte Hornets and Miami Heat were admitted in the 1988–89 season, and the Minnesota Timberwolves and Orlando Magic joined in 1989–90.

The original Miami starting lineup featured three veterans—point guard Rory Sparrow and forwards Billy Thompson and Pat Cummings—and two rookies, center Rony Seikaly and guard Kevin Edwards. On November 5, 1988, before a sold-out crowd in Miami Arena, head coach Ron Rothstein's squad took the floor against the Los Angeles Clippers for its inaugural NBA game, losing 111–91. It was the start of what

BECOMING THE HEAT

In the mid-1980s, when the NBA decided to expand from 23 teams to 27, Miami was an ideal candidate to receive an NBA franchise. The city was growing rapidly and in the midst of a cultural renaissance, as hundreds of local organizations in the arts and sciences were being founded and flourishing. With only the National Football League's Miami Dolphins in town, there was plenty of room for another professional sports team. So the Miami Sports and Exhibition Authority endorsed an investment group led by NBA Hall of Fame player Billy Cunningham, former sports agent Lewis Schaffel, and former Broadway producer Zev Buffman to begin wooing the NBA expansion committee. Between the allure of Miami and the formidable investment group, the city had a strong case. But it wasn't until Carnival Cruise Lines founder Ted Arison, who would become the club's majority owner, came on board with financial backing that the Miami group's proposal became irresistible. "Something big was happening in Miami," NBA commissioner David Stern remembered. "Something big in terms of the revitalization of the city. And we wanted to be part of that growth."

GLEN RICE

POSITION FORWARD
HEIGHT 6-FOOT-7
HEAT SEASONS
1989–95

As a boy in Flint, Michigan, Glen Rice spent much of his childhood at the playground with his brother, shooting baskets well into the night. After that, Rice always believed, "If I can shoot the ball at night, it shouldn't be any problem when the lights come on." During his 15 years in the NBA, the lights were on as Rice dropped in 18,336 points' worth of shots. Rice was a sharpshooter extraordinaire, but if a defender tried to play him tight, he could also blow past him with his explosive first step. Rice led the University of Michigan to a 1989 college championship with a tournament-record 184 total points before he was drafted by the Heat in 1989 as the fourth overall pick. The rangy forward was the pure scorer Miami had lacked. In 1991–92, he led the team in scoring, helping Miami make its very first playoff appearance. In his 5 seasons with the Heat, Rice set many club records, including a 56-point effort versus the Orlando Magic in 1995 that, until March 2014, stood as the highest single-game total by any Miami player in the regular season.

would be a painful season, even by first-year expansion team standards. The young Heat set an NBA record by losing their first 17 games. On December 14, the team finally pulled out an 89–88 road win against the Clippers for its first victory. Miami went on to finish with a league-worst 15–67 record.

The Heat had a fruitful 1989 NBA Draft, nabbing sharpshooting forward Glen Rice from the University of Michigan in the first round and crafty point guard Sherman Douglas from Syracuse University in the second. Although Rice and Douglas would have their share of productive seasons in Heat uniforms, Miami continued to struggle in 1989–90. The team improved its record by only three wins, going 18–64. Seikaly provided most of the season's highlights, averaging 16.6 points and 10.4 rebounds a game.

With the promising young trio of Douglas, Rice, and Seikaly, the Heat could attack opposing defenses in three ways. Douglas could penetrate from the point position and slash to the basket. Rice established his outside jump

shot as one of the most lethal in the game. And Seikaly provided muscle and combativeness down low. Miami improved to 24–58 in the 1990–91 campaign but remained in the Eastern Conference's Atlantic Division cellar. "The Heat have put together a nice group of kids," said coach Pat Riley, then with the Lakers. "If they give them some time to grow up, they'll have a good team."

RONY SEIKALY

**POSITION CENTER
HEIGHT 6-FOOT-11
HEAT SEASONS
1988–94**

Before their inaugural season, the Heat selected Rony Seikaly as the ninth overall pick in the 1988 NBA Draft. "I had a lot of high expectations for myself to put this franchise on my back," he said, "and I worked as hard as I could to help this franchise." Seikaly put in such effort, in fact, that he was named the NBA's Most Improved Player after the 1989–90 season. Nicknamed "The Spin Doctor" for his trademark spin moves in the post, Seikaly was integral in establishing a foundation for the fledgling franchise. By the time the center was traded away in 1994, Miami had made two playoff appearances and improved its record to 42–40. During his tenure with the Heat, Seikaly averaged double digits in both points and rebounds per game and developed a reputation as a ferocious competitor. Heat guard Rory Sparrow explained, "He didn't care what happened to him physically when he was in the battle." After retiring in 1999, Seikaly returned to Miami, bought season tickets, and became one of the Heat's biggest fans.

A TEAM GROWS UP

STEVE SMITH (LEFT) AND RONY SEIKALY (RIGHT) BROUGHT STRONG POSTSEASON DEFENSE.

n the 1991 NBA Draft, the Heat selected Steve Smith, a versatile guard from Michigan State University. A superb ball handler, Smith could play point guard, yet at 6-foot-7, he could also be a force under the basket. Smith filled the chinks in the Heat's armor, helping new coach Kevin Loughery lead Miami to a 38–44 record and the eighth seed in the 1992 Eastern Conference playoffs. Even though they were quickly dispatched by Michael Jordan and the Bulls, the Heat earned the distinction of becoming the first of the four expansion teams of the late '80s to appear in the postseason.

Early in the 1992–93 season, Smith went down with a knee injury, and Miami fell into a 13–27 hole. The young guard returned to the lineup at midseason, but the team finished the year just 36–46 and came up short of a return trip to the playoffs. Before the start of the next season,

17

PAT RILEY

COACH
HEAT SEASONS
1995–2003,
2005–08

Pat Riley was an NBA legend before he arrived in Miami, so it was of little surprise when he turned the Heat into an Eastern Conference powerhouse. Riley arrived in South Florida in 1995 after a 4-year stint in New York, where he put together 4 seasons of 50-plus wins and led the Knicks to the 1994 NBA Finals. During his 1981 to 1990 tenure with the Los Angeles Lakers, Riley had averaged 59 wins a season at the helm of legendary "Showtime" Lakers teams that included NBA greats Kareem Abdul-Jabbar, Magic Johnson, and James Worthy. Already respected as a coach and evaluator of talent, Riley made a name for himself in Miami as a shrewd trader in the front office as well, bringing All-Stars Shaquille O'Neal, Alonzo Mourning, and Tim Hardaway to town. Riley's slicked-back hair and Armani suits gave him an image as precise and polished as his managing style. Former Lakers general manager Jerry West summed Riley up by saying, "He's inventive. He makes good, quick decisions. He has tremendous belief in himself and his role. He has the perfect temperament."

Rice challenged his teammates. "We're not kids anymore," he said. "The fans have been patient with us. Now it's time to reward them."

The 1993–94 Heat answered their sharpshooter's call and finished 42–40, the franchise's first winning mark. Rice led the charge with 21.1 points per game. Entering the playoffs as the eighth seed, Miami faced the top-seeded Atlanta Hawks. In Game 1, the Heat came from behind in the fourth quarter to secure the franchise's first playoff win. Rice, Seikaly, and company pushed the heavily favored Hawks to a decisive Game 5 before losing the series.

espite the club's progress— having just run neck-and-neck with an Eastern Conference heavyweight in the playoffs— the Heat underwent a major overhaul in the 1994 off-season. Seikaly was traded to the Golden State Warriors for athletic forward Billy Owens, and Smith and forward Grant Long were sent to Atlanta in exchange for muscular center Kevin Willis. Coach Loughery moved to a position in the team's front office, and Alvin Gentry took his place as head coach.

Willis, a long-armed seven-footer, had consistently put up big numbers in Atlanta, and early on, Willis and Rice were one of the league's highest-scoring duos. Rice cemented his status as one of the league's best shooters, finishing 9th in the NBA in scoring (22.3 points per game) as he rained down scores of three-point bombs. Ultimately, though, the roster shake-up backfired. Willis was plagued by injury in the second half of the season, and the Heat ended the year a disappointing 32–50.

After that setback season, the Heat really shook things up. On September 2, 1995, Miami hired Pat Riley as the franchise's new president and head coach. Riley arrived with a most impressive resumé. As coach of the Lakers and the New York Knicks, Riley had won 4 NBA championships, taken his teams to the playoffs every year (13 straight), and won 50 or more games in each season as a head coach. "We're going to build this franchise into a winner the only way I know how," Riley told reporters when he arrived in Miami. "We're going to bring in the best players, and we'll work harder than anyone else."

Riley didn't waste any time bringing in the players he wanted. The first item on the coach's wish list was a franchise center. In Los Angeles and New York, Riley had built his teams around dominant centers Kareem Abdul-Jabbar and Patrick Ewing respectively. On the eve of the regular season, Riley landed one of the NBA's best big men when the Heat traded Rice, center Matt Geiger, and guard Khalid Reeves to the Hornets for All-Star center Alonzo Mourning. Guard Pete Myers and forward LeRon Ellis also came to Miami as part of the swap.

But Riley wasn't done. Midway through the 1995–96 season, he sent Willis and guard Bimbo Coles to the Warriors for forward Chris Gatling and lightning-quick point guard Tim Hardaway. After Riley's historic flurry of trades, the Heat were virtually unrecognizable; only one player from the previous year, forward Keith Askins, remained on the roster.

RORY SPARROW

THE EXPANSION CHAMPIONS

Because the Miami Heat and the Charlotte Hornets both entered the NBA as expansion teams in 1988, a rivalry blossomed between the two. The franchises built their rosters in contrasting fashion. The Hornets signed mostly veteran players in an effort to win quickly, while the Heat aimed to develop young players for the long haul. On February 17, 1989, the Hornets and Heat met for the first time in what would turn out to be a nail-biting expansion team showdown. Late in the game, which was played in Miami, Heat guard Rory Sparrow blocked a shot by Hornets guard Muggsy Bogues, who had broken into the open court for what seemed an easy layup. Sparrow also came up with a big three-point shot to tie the game at 100, and he put the Hornets away with a buzzer-beating turnaround shot from the free-throw line, sending the Miami crowd into a frenzy. Ira Winderman, a *Miami Sun-Sentinel* sportswriter, put the win in perspective, noting, "The Charlotte game was that first really emotional game for the fans where they had something special to celebrate."

ONE HOT RIVALRY

THE '90s SPARKED A FIERY RIVALRY BETWEEN THE HEAT AND THE CHICAGO BULLS.

The new-look Heat finished 42–40 in 1995–96 and kept Riley's streak of playoff appearances alive. In the postseason, they were swept in the first round by the 72–10 Bulls (who were on their way to claiming their fourth NBA crown in six seasons), but Miami fans were confident that their team was on the verge of greatness.

The Heat did indeed surge to new heights, capturing their first Atlantic Division title in 1996–97 with a 61–21 record. Two new additions, sturdy swingman Dan Majerle and big-bodied forward P. J. Brown, helped the Heat suffocate opponents on defense, while Hardaway and Mourning carried most of the scoring load. The Heat relied on their home-court advantage to win a five-game series versus the Magic in the opening round of the 1997 playoffs. In round two, the Heat met Riley's old team, the Knicks.

SHORT-HANDED BUT ON TARGET

In February 1996, coach Pat Riley and the Heat put together a blockbuster trade, sending five players to various teams to bring in point guard Tim Hardaway and four other players. Because of the timing of the trade, the Heat's newly acquired players could not make the trip to Miami in time for a face-off against the world champion Bulls. "It was a throwaway game to me," Riley said. "We had eight guys. We had to hustle guard Tony Smith in here quick just to be legal." Although they were overmatched and outnumbered, the Heat came out of the locker room on fire. Heat guard Rex Chapman in particular was in the zone, knocking down one three-pointer after another until the Heat had built a 26-point lead in the third quarter. When the Bulls made a late run, Chapman continued his hot shooting to preserve a 113–104 Miami victory. Chapman finished with a career-high 39 points, nailing 9 of his 10 three-point attempts. A stunned Coach Riley noted, "We still had ... Rex, and Rex just had one of those nights."

Heat broadcaster Jim Berry saw a fierce battle coming. "This was going to be a rivalry on so many levels," he later said. "It was Pat Riley against his old team. It was Alonzo Mourning versus Patrick Ewing."

The Knicks took a three-games-to-one lead, but momentum shifted in the Heat's favor in Game 5 when, during a tussle under the basket, Brown flipped Knicks guard Charlie Ward over his hip and into the crowd, and a melee ensued. When the skirmish ended, the Knicks had lost Ewing, Ward, and guard Allan Houston to suspensions for Game 6 and forward Larry

Johnson and guard John Starks for Game 7, while the Heat lost Brown for both games. The Heat won Game 5, and then—with the Knicks' best players in street clothes—Miami won the last two games and the series. The Heat advanced to their first Eastern Conference finals, only to fall to the Bulls in five games.

The Heat had high expectations going into their 10th-anniversary season. The team captured a second straight division title and met New York again in the first round of the playoffs. The Knicks came into the series still seething from the previous year's wrenching playoff defeat.

LEGENDARY COACH PAT RILEY DEMANDED GREATNESS OF ALL HIS PLAYERS.

ALONZO MOURNING

POSITION CENTER
HEIGHT 6-FOOT-10
HEAT SEASONS 1995–2002,
2004–08

When Pat Riley arrived in Miami, he believed that to have any chance of contending for the NBA championship, the Heat would need a dominant big man—an intimidator in the paint and a center with a soft touch around the bucket. Riley got his man in 1995 when he traded for Alonzo Mourning. Mourning, known to his teammates as "Zo," was a ferocious competitor. He not only supplied the Heat with points, rebounds, and blocked shots, but he was also the emotional leader and competitive heart of the team, putting an exclamation point on many of his biggest blocks and most crucial points with a reverberating battle cry. Mourning set the standard for work ethic in Miami, spending hours in the weight room in the off-season. On March 30, 2009, the Heat retired Mourning's number 33 jersey. As the jersey was raised to the rafters in a sold-out American Airlines Arena, Riley told Zo, "You have sacrificed more than any other player we've ever had in this franchise. And that's why we're raising these numbers right here, forever."

"IT MIGHT NOT HAVE BEEN THE MOST ARTISTIC, BUT FROM AN EFFORT STANDPOINT, FROM A DEFENSIVE STANDPOINT, FROM A COMPETITIVE STANDPOINT,... IT WAS SOME OF THE BEST BASKETBALL THAT'S EVER BEEN PLAYED."

— PAT RILEY ON THE RIVALRY WITH THE KNICKS

The rematch was a tense affair, and tempers flared in Game 4 between Mourning and the Knicks' Johnson—former teammates in Charlotte. This time, in a reversal of fortune, it was the Heat who lost one of their best players to a suspension. Without Mourning, the Heat lost the deciding Game 5 in a 98–81 rout.

The 1998–99 season brought good news to Eastern Conference contenders such as the Heat. Michael Jordan had retired, and Chicago's long stranglehold on the conference crown was finally over. At the end of a season shortened by a labor dispute between NBA players and owners, the Heat emerged with a 33–17 record and the top seed in the playoffs. Their first-round opponent was, once again, the Knicks. In the waning moments of the final game of the series, the Knicks' Houston threw up a running, one-handed shot that bounced high off the rim and then dropped in for a 78–77 New York win. The shot made the Knicks only the second eighth seed in the history of the NBA playoffs to defeat a number-one seed. "Life in basketball has a lot of suffering in it," Coach Riley said. "And we will suffer this one."

The Heat won a fourth consecutive division title in 1999–2000. Throughout the season, New York had nipped at Miami's heels for the division lead, and in round two of the playoffs, the archrivals faced off yet again. In another bruising series, the teams battled back and forth until the final buzzer of Game 7. With barely two minutes remaining in that deciding game, Hardaway hit a three-pointer to give the Heat an 82–81 advantage. But on the next possession, New York's Ewing beat Mourning to the baseline for a dunk, and the Knicks held on for an 83–82 win—New York's third straight playoff series victory over the Heat.

Between 1997 and 2000, the Heat and the Knicks had met in the playoffs four consecutive times, and each year, the series had come down to the last possible game. Packed with fights and last-second wins, the rivalry stands as one of the most intense in NBA history. Coach Riley summed the rivalry up best by saying, "It might not have been the most artistic, but from an effort standpoint, from a defensive standpoint, from a competitive standpoint, where you are not going to give your man anything and he's not going to give you anything, it was some of the best basketball that's ever been played."

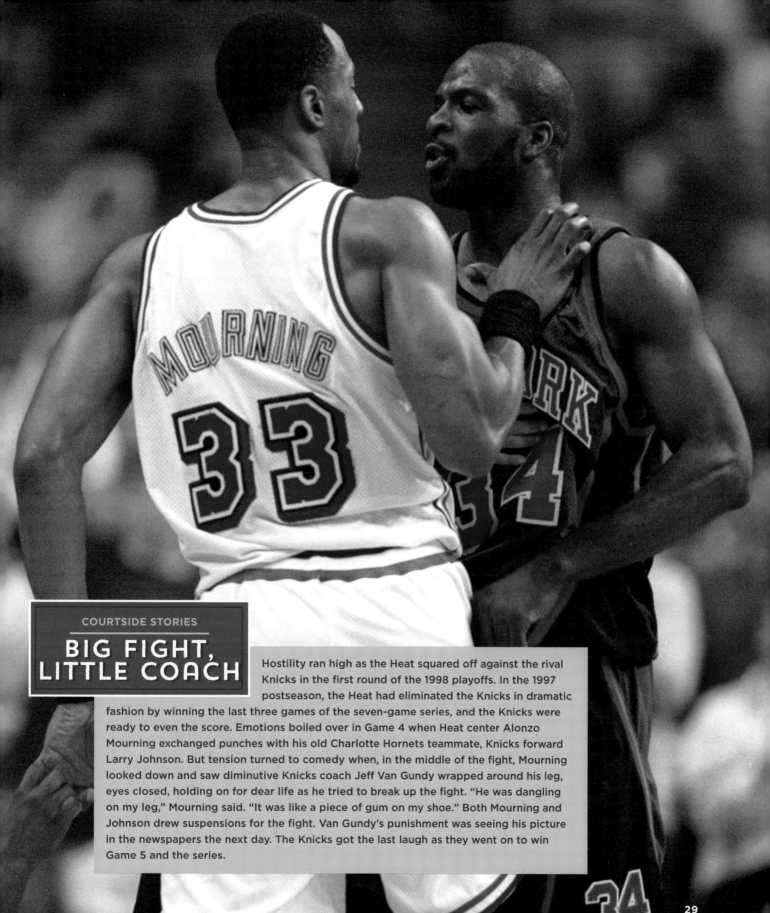

BIG FIGHT, LITTLE COACH

Hostility ran high as the Heat squared off against the rival Knicks in the first round of the 1998 playoffs. In the 1997 postseason, the Heat had eliminated the Knicks in dramatic fashion by winning the last three games of the seven-game series, and the Knicks were ready to even the score. Emotions boiled over in Game 4 when Heat center Alonzo Mourning exchanged punches with his old Charlotte Hornets teammate, Knicks forward Larry Johnson. But tension turned to comedy when, in the middle of the fight, Mourning looked down and saw diminutive Knicks coach Jeff Van Gundy wrapped around his leg, eyes closed, holding on for dear life as he tried to break up the fight. "He was dangling on my leg," Mourning said. "It was like a piece of gum on my shoe." Both Mourning and Johnson drew suspensions for the fight. Van Gundy's punishment was seeing his picture in the newspapers the next day. The Knicks got the last laugh as they went on to win Game 5 and the series.

TROPICAL TITLES

BRIAN GRANT AVERAGED A CAREER-BEST 15.2 POINTS PER GAME HIS FIRST MIAMI SEASON.

n 2000–01, Miami was the favorite to win the Eastern Conference. The team had bolstered its lineup, acquiring nimble guard Eddie Jones and rugged forwards Anthony Mason and Brian Grant, but bad news struck Miami just before the season when Mourning was diagnosed with a rare kidney disease—forcing "Zo" to miss the first 69 games of the season. His teammates, though, set out to prove that the Heat were more than just a one-man show. "Alonzo is our leader, but this is an opportunity for the rest of us to lead in his absence," said Majerle. "We won't quit, because we owe that to Zo." The Heat showed resilience by winning 50 games without their star center, and Riley became the first coach ever to advance to 19 consecutive NBA playoffs. Unfortunately, Miami was swept by Charlotte in the postseason's first round.

That started a downward spiral that lasted two seasons

ARTY OF THREE

The celebration had the feel of one that followed an NBA championship. But the only thing the Miami Heat had won on July 9, 2010, was that summer's free-agent competition. After re-signing their own star guard Dwyane Wade earlier that off-season and obtaining the great LeBron James from the Cleveland Cavaliers and forward Chris Bosh from the Toronto Raptors just a couple of days earlier, the Heat introduced the "Three Kings" to their fans. More than 13,000 screaming fans showed up to American Airlines Arena to see those players wearing Miami Heat uniforms for the first time. Together, they chanted, "Yes. We. Did!" as Wade, James, and Bosh walked out on the stage. "This is surpassing a dream come true," Wade said. "You always want to put yourself in the best position possible. To have an opportunity to team up with arguably the best trio to ever play the game of basketball is amazing." Asked if they would win a championship together, James predicted, "Not one, not two, not three, not four, not five, not six, not seven ... and when I say that I really believe it."

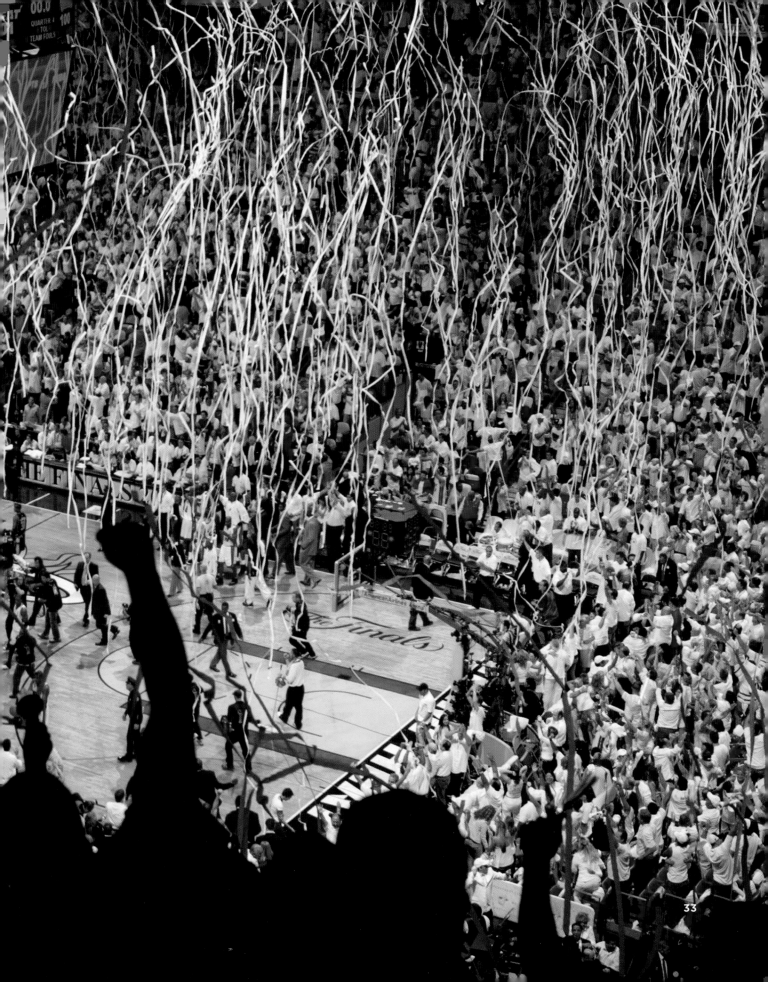

HIGH-SCORING EDDIE JONES ADJUSTED HIS GAME TO BETTER SUPPORT HIS TALENTED TEAMMATES.

and saw Riley's personal playoff streak end. In 2003, Mourning left town, and the rebuilding began. The Heat drafted highflying guard Dwyane Wade and signed multidimensional forward Lamar Odom as a free agent. Still, it would take another headline-making, Riley-engineered trade for the Heat to become an NBA powerhouse again.

On July 14, 2004, Miami made just such a trade, acquiring All-Star center and three-time NBA Finals Most Valuable Player (MVP) Shaquille O'Neal from the Lakers. The Heat paid a heavy price by giving up three players and a first-round draft pick, but Riley was confident

that O'Neal was the piece they needed in order to capture a title. "Today," he said, "the Miami Heat took a giant step forward in our continued pursuit of an NBA championship for the city of Miami and this franchise."

Miami then brought back a familiar face midway through 2004–05, reacquiring Alonzo Mourning from the New Jersey Nets to back up O'Neal. Wade, O'Neal, and Mourning powered the Heat to a 59–23 record and a playoff run to the 2005 Eastern Conference finals, where they faced the defending NBA champion Detroit Pistons. Although Wade played the series with a broken rib, and O'Neal was slowed by nagging

DWYANE WADE

POSITION GUARD
HEIGHT 6-FOOT-4
HEAT SEASONS
2003–PRESENT

Dwyane Wade grew up in Chicago watching Michael Jordan lead the Bulls to six NBA championships, and as soon as he joined the Heat in 2003, it became apparent he had picked up a few of Jordan's moves along the way. Like Jordan, Wade possessed unreal athleticism and showcased a lightning-quick first step. Once he beat his man, he had the ability to hit a short jumper, take the ball to the rim for the dunk, or dish to an open teammate. After Wade sliced through the tough Detroit defense early in the 2005 Eastern Conference finals, the Pistons began closing up the interior lanes in Game 4. Unable to penetrate to the basket, Wade struggled, and the Pistons dealt the Heat a painful defeat. The following off-season, Wade spent hours in the gym improving his outside shot and learning to move without the ball. The hard work paid off the next year, when the Heat won the 2006 NBA championship. Six years later, Wade's leadership helped propel Miami to another title.

SHAQUILLE O'NEAL POWERED TO THE HOOP USING HIS 7-FOOT-1 AND 325-POUND FRAME.

VERSATILE FORWARD
SHAWN MARION POSTED
229 POINTS DURING HIS
BRIEF STAY IN MIAMI.

MICHAEL BEASLEY HAD THE SMOOTH BALL-HANDLING SKILLS TO BEAT HIS DEFENDER OFF THE DRIBBLE.

injuries, Miami fought the Pistons tooth-and-nail all the way to the final minutes of an 88–82 loss in Game 7.

In the off-season, Riley added forwards Antoine Walker and James Posey and slick-passing point guard Jason Williams. With this retooled roster, Miami went 52–30 and made a return to the conference finals, where it again faced Detroit. Against the Pistons, Wade exploded to new heights of stardom. The vaunted Detroit defense had no answer for the quickness of the guard known as "Flash," and the Heat won the series in six games to advance to their first NBA Finals.

iami's prospects looked grim after the Heat lost the first two games of the 2006 Finals to star forward Dirk Nowitzki and the Dallas Mavericks. In the last six minutes of Game 3, though, Wade took over, engineering a comeback by calmly slicing through the Mavericks' defense and hitting one big shot after another. The Heat never looked back, capturing the NBA title with four straight wins. Wade was named Finals MVP, and Riley finally delivered Miami the championship he had promised. "The great Pat Riley told me we were going to win today," O'Neal said after the game. "I didn't have the best game. But D-Wade's been doing it all year. He's the best player ever."

Injuries cooled off Wade and the Heat over the next two seasons. Riley ended the Heat's Wade–Shaq era by trading O'Neal to the Phoenix Suns, and in 2007–08, just two seasons after winning the NBA championship, Miami finished with the league's worst record, 15–67.

Miami's only good fortune was that the horrible record gave it the second overall pick in the 2008 NBA Draft, which it used to land high-scoring, 6-foot-9 forward Michael Beasley. Miami also made a draft-day trade to acquire rookie point guard Mario Chalmers from the University of Kansas. Miami fans witnessed a change in leadership as well, as Erik Spoelstra was named the club's new head coach, and Riley focused exclusively on his role as team president.

When the 2008–09 season began, Wade made it clear that his injury woes were behind him as he averaged an NBA-best 30.2 points per game. Beasley and Chalmers put forth quality rookie efforts, and the Heat returned to the playoffs. It was a modest improvement, though,

FORWARD CHRIS BOSH AND HIS SUPERSTAR TEAMMATES OFTEN DISHED EACH OTHER NO-LOOK PASSES.

BIG MAN JERMAINE O'NEAL AVERAGED 13.6 POINTS PER GAME IN 2009–10.

as Miami was knocked out in the first round that year and then repeated the result in 2009–10.

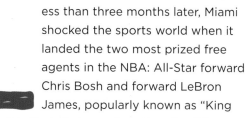

Less than three months later, Miami shocked the sports world when it landed the two most prized free agents in the NBA: All-Star forward Chris Bosh and forward LeBron James, popularly known as "King James." In their first year together, the "Big Three" of James, Wade, and Bosh carried the Heat all the way to the NBA Finals, but they fell short, losing in six games to the Mavericks. James came back stronger the next season

and was named MVP. More importantly, he excelled in the playoffs, averaging 30.3 points, 8.7 rebounds, and 6.7 assists. Miami edged the Boston Celtics in seven games in the Eastern Conference finals. In the series-clinching game, James scored 31 points, Wade had 23, and Bosh contributed 19 to the 101–88 Miami victory. From there, the Heat won their second NBA title, beating the Oklahoma City Thunder in five games. James was named Finals MVP. "Winning a championship, it's the reason that we all came here together," Wade said. "And I'm not just talking about Chris, LeBron, and myself. I'm talking about Shane Battier. I'm talking about

INTRODUCING...

LeBRON JAMES

POSITION FORWARD
HEIGHT 6-FOOT-8
HEAT SEASONS
2010–14

When LeBron James announced what team he would be playing for in 2010, nearly 10 million people tuned in to the nationally televised broadcast. Countless others also paid attention to what was known as "The Decision," curious to find out where the greatest basketball player of his generation and one of the biggest free-agent prizes in sports history would go. A gifted player who combined size and power with a soft scoring touch and savvy passing skills, James played his first seven NBA seasons with his "hometown" Cleveland Cavaliers. There, the Akron, Ohio, native earned two MVP awards and led the Cavs all the way to the NBA Finals in 2007. Three years later, when James said, "I'm going to take my talents to South Beach and join the Miami Heat," fans reacted differently. Those in Cleveland who wanted him to stay loyal to his home state were angry. But the folks in Miami were thrilled, especially when "King James" won two more MVP awards and led the Heat to back-to-back NBA championships in 2012 and 2013.

NOT JUST FOR SKATERS

With superstars such as Dwyane Wade, LeBron James, and Chris Bosh all on the same roster, sharing the ball is of the utmost importance in having success and winning championships. The Heat players have been so good at passing the ball to each other that they created a statistic to reflect those skills. Inspired by Miami's National Hockey League Florida Panthers, the Heat keep track of their "hockey assists" during each game. In hockey, up to two assists can be awarded for a goal, and each counts as a scoring point on the players' statistics. In basketball, however, just one assist can be awarded per basket. But to the Heat, those unofficial secondary assists are just as important to their high-powered offense, as they eventually lead to baskets by their talented scorers. "We're playing at a high level offensively, and it's because we have unselfish guys," James said. "We don't care who shoots, we don't care who passes. We're finding the open guy, and everyone on the floor is making plays. That's all that matters."

Mike Miller. I'm talking about all these guys."

The Heat were even better the following season. The Big Three led the squad to an NBA-best 66–16 record, a mark that included an amazing 27-game winning streak. That streak was just 6 victories shy of the NBA record of 33 set by the 1971–72 Lakers. "It's one of the best this league has ever seen," James said of Miami's streak. James won his fourth MVP award after the season and took his team to glory for the second straight year. "Everything. It took everything we had as a team," Dwyane Wade said. "We're a resilient team. We did whatever it took."

In 2013–14, the Heat discovered that being the defending champions came with its own challenges, namely high expectations and opponents who were eager to loosen Miami's grip on the title. The Heat held on tight to the top of the Eastern Conference until a late-season losing streak showed even the stars' vulnerability. "It's the toughest season we've had since Year One just because of everything that comes with it," said James. "We have to find our own motivation every single night. It's not always about our opponent. It's about ourselves, too."

As it entered the playoffs, Miami's superstars—especially James—indeed made the postseason about themselves, dominating the news cycles, even when they were losing games. But the most crushing of those losses didn't occur until the NBA Finals, when the San Antonio Spurs stampeded over Miami in a show of offensive prowess over five games. Miami's Coach Spoelstra gave the Spurs credit on their championship style of play without qualm. "They played exquisite basketball … and they were the better team. There's no other way to say it." After the Finals, a weary Battier announced his retirement, James decided to return home to the Cavaliers a few weeks later, and fans were left to wonder what would become of the crew in 2014-15.

Despite its short history, the Miami Heat quickly found a place amid the glitzy lifestyle of southern Florida. Great playoff games, a legendary coach, and several future Hall-of-Famers have made the franchise as important to Miami as the Atlantic Ocean. And with three championships to their name, the Heat have made that coast even more golden.

CHRIS BOSH (CENTER) AND LeBRON JAMES (RIGHT) HELPED THE HEAT BUILD AN NBA DYNASTY.

INDEX

American Airlines Arena 27, 32

Askins, Keith 20

Battier, Shane 42, 45

Beasley, Michael 39

Bosh, Chris 32, 42, 44

Brown, P. J. 23, 25

Chalmers, Mario 39

Chapman, Rex 24

Coles, Bimbo 20

Cummings, Pat 10

division championships 23, 25, 28

Douglas, Sherman 14

Eastern Conference finals 25, 34, 35, 39, 42

Edwards, Kevin 10

Ellis, LeRon 20

Gatling, Chris 20

Geiger, Matt 20

Gentry, Alvin 20

Grant, Brian 31

Hardaway, Tim 18, 20, 23, 24, 28

James, LeBron 32, 42, 43, 44, 45

Jones, Eddie 31

Long, Grant 20

Loughery, Kevin 17, 20

Majerle, Dan 23, 31

Mason, Anthony 31

Miami Arena 10

Miller, Mike 45

Most Improved Player award 15

Most Valuable Player award 42,

43, 45

Mourning, Alonzo 18, 20, 23, 25, 27, 28, 29, 31, 34

Myers, Pete 20

NBA championships 32, 35, 39, 42, 43, 45

NBA Finals 39, 42, 45

NBA records 14

Odom, Lamar 34

O'Neal, Shaquille 18, 34, 35, 39

Owens, Billy 20

playoffs 12, 15, 17, 20, 23, 25, 28, 29, 31, 34, 35, 39, 42, 45

Posey, James 39

Reeves, Khalid 20

retired numbers 27

Rice, Glen 12, 14, 20

Riley, Pat 14, 18, 20, 23, 24, 25, 27, 28, 31, 34, 39

Rothstein, Ron 10

Seikaly, Rony 10, 14, 15, 20

Smith, Steve 17, 20

Smith, Tony 24

Sparrow, Rory 10, 15, 21

Spoelstra, Erik 39, 45

team name 9–10

team records 14, 15, 17, 20, 23, 28, 34, 39, 45

Thompson, Billy 10

Wade, Dwyane 32, 34, 35, 39, 42, 44, 45

Walker, Antoine 39

Williams, Jason 39

Willis, Kevin 20